NOODLEHEAD'S
Step-by-Step
SHOEBOX BILL PAYING METHOD

MAKE YOUR LIFE SIMPLER

ARLEEN WOLF

Publisher

Noodlehead's Step-by-Step Shoebox Bill Paying Method

Copyright @2021 by Arleen Wolf

Available online at:
www.Amazon.com

Library of Congress Cataloging Data

Noodlehead's Step-by-Step Shoebox Bill Paying Method / Arleen Wolf

ISBN: 9798459523546

Personal Finance for Young Adults / Financial Literacy

Noodlehead's Method helps Young Adults and Teens to become financially responsible and independent. It helps them to understand how and why to save money, spend money wisely and pay bills. The Method is clear, concise and fun and easy to follow.

Design: Asa Shatikin at shebangdesign.com

Noodlehead photo: Chris Watkins at chriswatkinsphoto.com

Printed in the United States of America

To my sons, Joshua and Asa.
I see you rolling your eyes.

CONTENTS

Prologue 6

INTRODUCTION

Getting Started 9

ABOUT MONEY

The Money Birds and the Money Bees 10

GETTING ORGANIZED

Get a Shoebox................................. 13
Get a Checking Account and a Savings Account 14
Paying Bills Online 15
Look at Your Monthly Bills 17
The Plastic Card 18
Decide When You're Going to Pay Your Bills 20
If You Get Paid Once a Month 22
If You Get Paid Twice a Month 24
If You Get Paid Every Week 26
Some Suggestions About How to Save Money 27

THE METHOD

Step by Step 28
How to Write a Check 34
How to Endorse a Check 37
How to Address an Envelope.................... 38
Clean it Out and Wrap It Up 40

Prologue

How this book began...

A young woman walked into the Emergency Room one Friday night and said that she was feeling scared and depressed. The ER docs spoke with her decided that it would be a good idea if she stayed in the hospital for a few days, so that she could be kept safe and get some counseling.

When she came up to the Psych Unit, where I was working as a nurse, I had a chance to talk to her and find out what had brought her to the hospital.

She told me that she was a freshman at the University and had never been away from home before. She lived off-campus with a roommate, but they hadn't become friends, and she felt lonely and overwhelmed.

I asked her what brought her to the hospital on that night and she said the final straw was having the electricity turned off in their apartment.

"Why was the electricity turned off?" I asked.
"Because I didn't pay the bill." she said.
"Why didn't you pay the bill?"
"I don't know how to pay bills." she said.
I told her that I would be working on the unit all

weekend and I would be glad to teach her how to pay bills, if she wanted to learn.

She seemed appreciative of the offer, and the next day I sat with her and taught her how to pay bills, the way my mother, who was a bookkeeper, had taught me. After that weekend, when there were a few students on the unit (usually just before midterms and finals), I would ask them if they wanted to learn how to pay bills and manage money and they always seemed interested.

After a while, the "bill paying group" became a regular event and more and more patients came to the group, then staff members began showing up and people started asking me to hold the group more and more often.

I was asked, by the medical director, to write an outline of what we talked about, thinking that, when I wasn't there, one of the other staff members could run the group.

That outline was the beginning of *Noodlehead's Step-by-Step Shoebox Bill Paying Method*.

P.S. The young woman was in a much better frame of mind after a weekend in the hospital. She was discharged with follow-up appointments for outpatient therapy. I never met her again, but I will never forget her and am grateful that we met.

INTRODUCTION

My grandmother used to call me Noodlehead because I would never let anyone cut my hair. So she said it looked like noodles. And because I have wacky adventures.

But inside this Noodlehead is a very organized brain. When this brain was plunged into the adult world of bills and debts, it devised a simple method for taking care of them.

I have taught this method to many people who are eternally grateful and jump for joy! My accountant wants to have a statue of me placed in the middle of town as a monument to good record-keeping.

Welcome to the world of *finance à la Noodlehead*.

CHAPTER ONE
ABOUT MONEY

Did anyone ever tell you about the money birds and the money bees? No, they did not. Money is a taboo subject in our culture. People go on TV and even write books about their sexual exploits, but ask them what their hourly wage is and their lips are sealed.

I'm going to share one of life's secrets with you.

Money is only a tool.

It's useful for getting our basic needs met like food, shelter and clothing. And beyond that, it helps us get the things we want: trips to Paris, motorcycles, fancy shoes, etc.…

I can't tell you how to make money, but try doing something that you like or try liking what you do. Life should be happy and serene, but it isn't when your bills aren't paid.

So, pay your bills. I'll show you how.

CHAPTER TWO

GETTING ORGANIZED

GET A SHOEBOX

If you have any paper receipts or bills, keep them in your shoebox. When you walk into your home with your mail, put any bills you have gotten into the box. Put anything that has to do with money, like receipts and tax forms, into the box. Keep the shoebox in a place that's easy to reach when you walk into the house.

Here are some things that I keep in my shoebox:

- Envelopes
- Stamps
- A pen
- A small notebook
- My checkbook

GET A CHECKING ACCOUNT *AND* A SAVINGS ACCOUNT

Open a checking and a savings account, either at a bank or a credit union. I use a local Credit Union. Like a bank, a credit union provides credit and other financial services to its members. Unlike a bank, a credit union is a not-for-profit institution that is owned by its members.

I've never paid check fees or service fees and most of the tellers at the Credit Union know me. Many employees offer "Direct Deposit" to employees. You can have your paycheck deposited right into your checking account (no standing in line on payday).

You can choose to have some of your money put directly into your savings account or even a retirement plan at work. Just ten dollars a week, in your savings account, turns into $520 a year - and you don't even feel it when it's taken right out of your check ... and it's in your savings account if you're in a pinch.

As you start to earn more money you can put more money into savings. I use the debit card from the Credit Union to pay for most things and to get cash from the ATM.

I have a Plastic Card from a big bank. I use it when I buy things online so that I don't have to put the information about my Credit Union account on line. It also makes it easy to keep track of the few things I buy online, in case there's a problem with something I've bought.

PAYING BILLS ONLINE

Most bills can be paid online but in some cases you may need to pay with a check.

So first, you have to set up your online account at your credit union or bank. When you log on to your bank site, your home page will have a button for **Bill Pay**.

If you click on **Bill Pay** (or whatever option your bank calls it) to pay bills, you can set it up so that you can pay each monthly bill through the bank's web site.

$ NOODLEHEAD'S CREDIT UNION			
	HOME	**My Checking** Available Balance: $1,000,000.00	My Savings: Available Balance: $1,000.00
	TRANSFERS		
>>>>>>>>>>>>>>>	**BILL PAY**		
	eDOCUMENTS		
	SERVICES		
	MESSAGES		
	HELP		
	LOG OFF		

My Credit Union does not charge extra for this service.

I don't do any automatic payments. That way I have control over when and how to pay each bill.

Pay to:	Pay from:	Amount:	Payment date:	Actions:
Rent	Checking Account	$$$	July 22, 2020	**PAY**
Utilities	Checking Account	$$$	July 3, 2020	**PAY**
Phone	Checking Account	$$$	July 22, 2020	**PAY**
Car Insurance	Checking Account	$$$	July 22, 2020	**PAY**
PlasticCard	Checking Account	$$$	July 3, 2020	**PAY**
Car	Checking Account	$$$	July 22, 2020	**PAY**

Some companies charge a fee if you pay through their website and they want you to do Automatic Payments. I recommend avoiding their fee and setting up payments through your bank.

The company will send the bill by email or snail mail. If it's by snail mail, open the envelope, write the 'due date' on the front of the envelope and put it in the shoebox.

LOOK AT YOUR MONTHLY BILLS

Make a list like this:

Bill	Due	Amount
Rent	1st	$500
Utilities	26th	$75
Phone	29th	$75
Car Insurance	8th	$75
PlasticCard	25th	$50
Car	22nd	$200

If those are your bills, they add up to a whopping $975.

That doesn't include food, clothing or anything fun. This is a good time to decide if you can cut back on some expenses.

THE PLASTIC CARD

Pay it off as fast as you can. Use it only when you absolutely have to.

If you can't afford to buy something, don't try to convince yourself that you can. If you want a sweater that costs $100 and you have $30 in the bank and $10 in your pocket, then you can't afford it… and you're lying to yourself if you think you can.

You'll be surprised at how much you have that you don't really need and how much easier life is when you don't have a lot of stuff. Simplifying your life and being free of debt feels good.

DECIDE WHEN YOU'RE GOING TO PAY YOUR BILLS

If you're lucky enough to have lots of money in the bank all the time, then pay your bills as soon as you get them.

Most of us don't have lots of money in the bank. We live paycheck-to-paycheck and have to do some planning. At first, this takes some thought and preparation but, after just a couple of times, it becomes easy as pie.

Look at the "Due by" date on each bill.

Some companies give you a "grace period" before they start charging service fees, high interest rates or reconnection fees. Extra fees are a waste of your money, so paying bills on or before the 'due date' is smart.

Some bills are due at the beginning of the month.
Some bills are due at the end of the month.

If you get paid once a month, you can pay your bills once a month.

If you get paid twice a month, you can separate your bill according to the 'due date" and pay them twice a month.

If you get paid every week, you can still divide your bills up and just pay them once or twice a month.

IF YOU GET PAID ONCE A MONTH

If you get paid once a month, let's say on the 1st of the month, choose one day during the 1st week of the month to pay all of the bills.

Maybe Thursdays are kind of do-nothing days. So set aside the 1st Thursday of each month and ***just pay them on Thursday***.

For example, if you get paid on January 1st and the 1st falls on a Monday, then pay your bills on Thursday, the 4th.

If you get paid on February 1st and it falls on a Thursday, make sure that your bills are in the mail before the next Thursday rolls around.

Bill	Due	Amount	Paid Jan 4
Rent (for Feb)	1 st	500	x
Electric	26th	100	x
Phone	29th	50	x
Car Insurance	8th	75	x
PlasticCard	25th	50	x
Car	22nd	200	x

If you pay your bills this way, let's say on January 4th, then all your bills will be paid on time and you'll feel good.

You would be paying February's rent early. Sometimes this seems counter-intuitive. Most of us like to wait until the last minute to pay the rent, but there are some advantages to paying early.

One advantage is that you will have the peace of mind of knowing that the rent is paid and another is that if you decide to move and you have to give 30 days notice, you're all paid up and won't have to worry about the last month's rent. You'll be able to use what money you have for moving and other expenses.

IF YOU GET PAID TWICE A MONTH

Take a look at your list of bills. You can divide them up and pay them twice a month. Here's en example of how to do it if you get paid every other Friday:

			January			
Sun	Mon	Tues	Wed	Thurs	Fri	Sat
1	2	3	4	5	Payday 6	7
8	9	10	11	12	13	14
15	16	17	18	19	Payday 20	21
22	23	24	25	26	27	28
29	30					

Take a look at the "due date" on your bills. You can split them up and pay them like this:

Bill	Due	Amount	Paid Jan 6th	Paid Jan 20th
Rent (for Feb	1st	500		X
Electric	26th	100	X	
Phone	29th	50	X	
Car Insurance	8th	75		X
PlasticCard	25th	50	X	
Car	22nd	200	X	

If you divide them up this way, you'll have your bills paid on time. The amounts are divided up pretty evenly, so you don't have to spend all of your paycheck at once.

The Rent and Car Insurance add up to $575 and the rest of the bills add up to $400. You don't have to pay them on payday. You can relax on the weekend and choose a day during the week that works for you...like every other Monday.

Just be consistent and **_do it_**.

IF YOU GET PAID EVERY WEEK

Divide them up any way that's comfortable for you.

Sun	Mon	Tues	Wed	Thurs	Fri	Sat
			January			
	1	2	3	4	5 Payday 6	7
8	9	10	11	12	Payday 13	14
15	16	17	18	19	Payday 20	21
22	23	24	25	26	Payday 27	28
29	30					

You can pay the bills once a month, twice a month or once a week:

Bill	Due	Amount	Paid Jan 6	Paid Jan 13	Paid Jan 20	Paid Jan 27
Rent (for Feb)	1st	500			X	
Electric	26th	100		X		
Phone	29th	50		X		
Car Insurance	8th	75				X
PlastiCard	25th	50		X		
Car	22nd	200	X			

SOME SUGGESTIONS ABOUT HOW TO SAVE MONEY

Buy only what you *need*...not what you want.

If you see something you *gotta have*, resist it for a week. If the passion...and the something...is gone in 7 days then you just saved money and you managed to live without it for 7 days. You probably could live without it longer.

If the passion is still there in a week, then it may be something you'll enjoy for a long time. If you can afford it...*go for it*.

Sneak money out of your paycheck. Put it in savings, a retirement plan, a sock drawer, a piggy bank...whatever works for you.

After you have what you *need*, you can get what you *want*. If your bills are $1310.00 a month and you're only earning or living on $1200.00 a month, now is the time to take a look at how you can cut back on expenses... getting a roommate, a cheaper car, a bicycle, a part time job or any creative way you can think of to take in more money than you pay out.

Treat yourself kindly. That makes everything easier...

Now let's pay the bills. Step By Step.

CHAPTER THREE
THE METHOD

1. GET YOUR SHOEBOX

2. PICK A PLACE THAT'S CONVENIENT AND COMFORTABLE

Sometimes I sit on the couch and watch Judge Judy. I don't have to pay too much attention to the program and I've learned a lot, like:

- Don't move in with someone you've met at a bar and have known for less than 24 hours.
- Don't pay anyone's bail.
- Don't loan money to friends or family, unless you don't need it back.
- Don't date anyone who is married or has been divorced for less than a year.

- Don't cosign a loan for anyone.
- Don't buy a car or house with anyone, unless you're married to them and are very, very happy.

If you don't have a laptop, and you're paying online, then you have to sit at your desktop. If you're paying with checks, you can sit anywhere…and we'll get to paying by check in a little bit.

3. GATHER ALL YOUR BILLS

Get your shoebox, a bag for trash, something to sip and munch on, and put them on the table. Remember that all the steps get easier after you've done them a the few times.

Paying bills will never be as much fun as doing the Shiggy or the Macarena but you will feel good when you're finished.

4. KNOW YOUR BALANCE

You have to know what you've got in your checking account before you start paying your bills.

Just looking at your balance on your account's website or at an ATM is not always helpful…because they don't always include your latest trip to the ATM or what you paid for lunch with your debit card or outstanding bills that you've paid but have not been transferred out of your account yet.

Thanks to modern technology, you can go onto your Credit Union or bank website and check:

- your balance +
- outstanding payments
- if your lunch has been deducted from your account

The ATM will give you your balance, but not tell you if everything you've spent has been deducted.

Write your bank account balance on a piece of paper or on your computer calculator…or both.

5. PAY ONLINE

If you have a paper bill, open it up. Look at the Balance and the Due Date.

If the Balance is too high or overdue, I'll tell you what to do in a minute.

If you're okay with the Balance and the Due Date, then go to Bill Pay on your banking website and pay it.

You are the Pay*er* and the person or company you are giving your money to is the Pay*ee*.

The site will walk you through the setting up each Payee and will let you know when the money will be transferred.

When you are setting up your Payees, make sure you use the address on the bill that says **Make Payments to:** and not the Customer Service or Return Address of the company.

Deduct the amount of the bill from your Account Balance… and keep going until all the bills, that are due at this time, are paid.

Each bill will take a day or more to be processed and get to the Payee. It won't be deducted from your Account Balance until it's paid. That means that if your Account Balance is $500 and you pay a $100 bill, your Balance will still show $500 on your bank Home Page, so you have to be smart and keep track of your Balance.

If there's a problem with the bill, or if it's overdue…

Corporations and businesses don't want your property or to turn off your service and lose you as a customer. They want your Money. Don't be shy about calling and negotiating for a lower rate, a payment plan or an extension date for your payment.

Customer Service reps are people like us, and have the same problems paying their bills as the rest of us. They have to deal with angry people all day, so being nice and courteous will go a long way.

I have pool service with a small business and my Credit Union sends a check to The Pool Guy every month. It takes about a week for The Pool Guy to get the check. When I go to the Home page on my Credit Union site, I can check to see that the payment has been made and click onto the payment to view a copy of the bank check that was sent.

If The Pool Guy ever sues me, and we have to go to Hollywood and stand before Judge Judy, I can bring a print out of the check and my bank statement to prove that he was paid. Even though the Credit Union site keeps track of my transactions, I keep track of the bills I've paid with a chart like this:

	January	February	March	April	May	June
Rent						
Utilities						
Phone						
Insurance						
PlastiCard						
Car						

I just fill in the box after I pay the bill and change the headings every six months.

HOW TO WRITE A CHECK

There may be times when you have to write a check. Some businesses are *Cash Only* to save the money that the credit card companies charge for each transaction.

Some of the finest restaurants in my neighborhood take only cash or checks.

There are instructions that come with your checks, but there are some things that you should know to make writing checks convenient for you, as well as the check's recipient.

Checks look like this:

Your Name	Check No.
Address	
Phone Number	_____
	Date
Pay to the order of _____	$ _____
_____ Dollars	
Friendly Credit Union	
For _____	_____
7:1234987654 78:	12387600 2266

HERE'S HOW TO WRITE A CHECK, STEP-BY-STEP:

1. Write the date on the check.
2. Write the name of the person or company you are paying.
3. Write the amount in numbers, like this: $212.54.
4. Write the amount in words: Two hundred twelve and 54/100 (use fractions for the less than dollar amount. If you say the amount to yourself while you're writing it, it's easier to write… especially if it's a large mount of money, like, "Two hundred twelve dollars and 54 cents.") Make sure the whole line is filled up – so no one can change the amount you've written.
5. Write down what the check is for. (If you are ever sued and have face Judge Judy, she's going to want to see the cancelled check to prove, for instance, that you paid your friend's idiot boyfriend's bail…but you won't do that, will you?) Write "Loan for Billy the Idiot's bail" in the Memo line. Write the purpose of Every check in the Memo line, even if it's just an ordinary bill…just to cover yourself.
6. Sign the check.
7. Keep track of the number. You can write it in the ledger part of the checkbook and it will also be recorded on the copy page in your checkbook and in your bank statement.

Your check should wind up looking something like this:

```
Your Name                                    Check #3014
Address                                      April 2, 2042
Phone Number                                         Date

Pay to the
order of    William Teller                        $ 212.54
         Two hundred twelve and 54/100————————   Dollars

Friendly Credit Union
For  Loan for rent                          Noodlehead

7:1234987654 78:   12387600  3014
```

The numbers on the bottom of the check help to identify the financial institution and the account.

The first set of numbers are called the Routing Numbers. They identify the financial institution associated with the check, the next numbers are the account identification numbers and the last set of numbers are the check number.

HOW TO ENDORSE A CHECK:

When you get a check from someone, you have to endorse it, sign your name on the back of the check, if you want to deposit it or cash it.

If you want to deposit it, sign your name on the top line and write "*For Deposit*" and your account number on the next line.

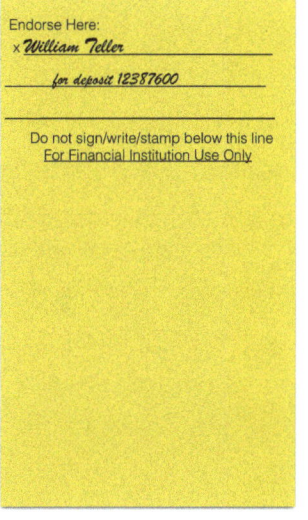

HOW TO ADDRESS AN ENVELOPE

You can pay all your bills by check… the advantage is that you don't put your info onto the internet, but you have to make sure that you put the check in an envelope, stamp it, write your return address and mail it.

You can also go to your bank or credit union and get a "bank check" made out to someone you want to give money to… they're free at my Credit Union… and you can send it like a regular check. The bank gives you the check, with a receipt attached. You can keep the receipt in the shoebox.

If you're not paying on line, most businesses send out their bills with a return envelope that is already addressed to them. Often the postage has already been paid.

Other companies… like the company that takes care of my lawn and garden… just send a bill every month and I have to send them a check, address the envelope and put a stamp on it.

Sometime or other, you'll have to send a check or something through the mail, so you might as well do it right.

The business's address goes front and center on the envelope, your return address in the upper left hand corner.

If you get a bill that includes a return envelope with a clear window, make sure the company's address is showing in the window. (I know, I know…but I've made that mistake at least once).

I love getting notes and thank you cards from friends and family and I'll bet you do, too. I know we don't do a lot of letter writing these days, but you should know how to do it… and you could keep some 'Thank you' notes and beautiful stamps in your shoebox, just to let people know you are grateful for their gifts to you. You can send a card for no reason at all… just to keep in contact with someone you care about.

CLEAN IT OUT AND WRAP IT UP

If you pay taxes, when you get back your tax return, file it away in an envelope with any important papers that are still in the shoebox.

If you don't pay taxes, at the end of the year, put all the receipts and papers from the shoebox into an envelope.

Write the year on the envelope and put it in a drawer or another shoebox.

Larry, my accountant, says that if you're like most people, and don't own your own business you should save a record of your expenses, and your tax returns, for 3 to 5 years.

If you own a business, save the records for 7 years…in case you're ever audited by the IRS, which is about as likely for most of us as winning the lottery.

Thank you for trying the *Noodlehead Method*. I'm very grateful for all the people, things and serenity that I have in my life and wish all those things for you, as well.

Please get in touch if you have questions or comments.
Email: *NoodleheadShoebox@gmail.com*

Arleen Wolf was born and raised in Brooklyn. She is a retired Psychiatric Nurse, living a serene and debt-free life in Gainesville, Florida.

www.ingramcontent.com/pod-product-compliance
Lightning Source LLC
Chambersburg PA
CBHW040251220526
45473CB00001B/445